Fossils and Feathers

DINOSAURS

Fossils and Feathers

MK REED   JOE FLOOD

:01
First Second
New York

First Second

Text copyright © 2016 by MK Reed
Illustrations copyright © 2016 by Joe Flood

Drawn with a Staedtler .07 mm mechanical pencil with Pilot Eno blue and light blue lead, inked with Dr Ph Martin's black India ink using a Raphael #8404 size 1 kolinsky sable brush and Nikko crow quill on Strathmore 500 series 2ply Vellum Bristol. Backgrounds colored with Schminke water colors on Farbriano Artistico paper. Remaining art colored digitally with Photoshop using Kyle Webster's digital brushes. Lettered in Comicrazy.

Published by First Second
First Second is an imprint of Roaring Brook Press,
a division of Holtzbrinck Publishing Holdings Limited Partnership
120 Broadway, New York, NY 10271
Cataloging-in-Publication Data is on file at the Library of Congress.

Paperback ISBN 978-1-62672-143-2
Hardcover ISBN 978-1-62672-144-9

Our books may be purchased in bulk for promotional, educational, or business use. Please contact your local bookseller or the Macmillan Corporate and Premium Sales Department at (800) 221-7945 ext. 5442 or by e-mail at MacmillanSpecialMarkets@macmillan.com.

FIRST

EDITION

First edition 2016
Book design by John Green

Printed in China by Toppan Leefung Printing Ltd., Dongguan City, Guandong Province
20 19 18 17 16 15 14 13 12 11

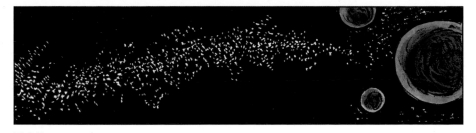

When I was a kid, I drew a picture of the dinosaur *Deinonychus*. This wasn't unusual for me. I loved dinosaurs by the time I could hold a pencil. I remember that particular *Deinonychus* so well because of how hard I tried to be imaginative when drawing it.

Why did this drawing require all the powers of my imagination? Because my *Deinonychus* had stripes! More shocking than that: the stripes were blue! Every dinosaur in every picture book I had ever seen was green, gray, or brown. I felt like a madman as I pulled the blue crayon from its box.

Looking back now, I know that I didn't go too far. In fact, I didn't go far enough. In all the years since I drew that picture, I've had one idea reinforced over and over: dinosaurs are fantastic.

The word "fantastic" literally means "appearing as if conceived from an unrestrained imagination." The most important discovery from the last few decades of paleontology is that we restrain our imaginations too much when we think about dinosaurs. In my wildest dreams I never dared to imagine the fuzzy coat on *Yutyrannus*, the buckteeth of *Incisivosaurus*, the comb-over on *Kosmoceratops*, the spiny neck of *Amargasaurus*, or *Microraptor*'s winged legs.

Go look up the most recent drawings of *Deinocheirus*. I'll bet your unrestrained imagination didn't see that one coming. No one's did.

The incredible new findings keep coming. Soft tissue in tyrannosaur bones and sauropod eggs. Color pigments in dromaeosaur feathers and hadrosaur scales. Burrowing ornithopods. Aquatic spinosaurs. Arctic dinosaurs. Antarctic dinosaurs. With each new discovery, we learn just how much we'd been restraining the way we imagined dinosaurs.

You might ask: Are we still restraining our imaginations when we think about dinosaurs? What fantastic new fact will literally rise up out of the Earth tomorrow? As you'll see, these are questions that paleontologists have been asking for centuries.

Reading their stories teaches us not only how dinosaurs lived, but also how we live.

We usually think of discovery as a process that limits possibilities. Think about looking for something—say, a dinosaur toy—in a messy room. When you start your search, you imagine that the toy might be in a number of different places: maybe under the bed or behind the dresser or buried under a bunch of other toys. But as you search, you eliminate possibilities. Once you discover where the toy is, you stop imagining other places it might be. This normal sort of discovery—discovery by process of elimination—is the kind that restrains our imaginations.

When I drew that *Deinonychus*, I wished that I could encounter a living dinosaur. I would sit in the backseat of my parents' car, searching in the passing trees for a glimpse of a dinosaur. I thought I'd see one if I could just find the right way to look. But even then, I believed finding a living dinosaur was just a fantasy.

Many years later, I took a class about the science and philosophy of evolution. The teacher had promised that I would learn about dinosaurs. And I did. I found out about a truly fantastic discovery, one that you'll read about later in this book. I learned that there are living dinosaurs that survived extinction. We call them "birds."

This discovery gave me new places to look for dinosaurs. I could look up from the rocks under my feet. I could look in a pond or on a tree branch or up in the sky. I had found the right way to look, and it changed the way I saw birds and the way I saw dinosaurs. It changed the way I saw everything.

The lesson that MK Reed and Joe Flood teach in this book is that scientific discovery is very different from normal discovery. Rather than limiting our imaginations, scientific discovery lets us imagine more about the world around us. Three hundred years ago, no one knew about dinosaurs at all. Two hundred years ago, no one knew that dinosaurs had lived on every continent. One hundred years ago, no one knew that the continents themselves moved around. Those discoveries changed the way we understand our world. Someday, discoveries you make could unleash our imaginations, too. That is what science does: it shows us how fantastic the world can be.

We now imagine dinosaurs with feathers. We imagine them with colorful stripes. By the time you reach the back cover of this book, you'll imagine them in ways you've never imagined them before.

In this book, you'll find plenty of dinosaurs drawn the way today's paleontologists imagine them. One of those dinosaurs is an up-to-date *Deinonychus*. Joe Flood has drawn the animal covered in feathers, stalking the middle ground between modern reptiles and birds. If my younger counterpart thought himself a madman for pulling out that blue crayon, then what would he say about Joe?

I can say this much now: Joe's art and MK Reed's words are just as fantastic as the animals that served as their inspiration. Their balance of science, philosophy, and history is informative, funny, and, above all, imaginative. The spirit of discovery hovers over each page.

Remember that as you read this book. Keep it in mind as you lean in closer to the page to take in new details in the *Rhinorex* herds, or when you pause to digest the idea that *T. rex* might have had feathers. The spirit of discovery lies in finding what is fantastic. As you read, the spirit of discovery lies in you.

Sometimes people say that your imagination flies once it's set free. When you turn this page, you'll begin to see that this is true. Let your imagination soar. You will find the fantastic. You will be among the dinosaurs.

—Leonard Finkelman, Ph.D.
Assistant Professor in Philosophy of Science, Linfield College

For 165 million years, dinosaurs walked the Earth.

...they mysteriously disappeared.

Except for their bones. And eggs. And some other things.

Some of these remains were preserved in rock, recording parts of their lives.

Humans evolved 66 million years after the dinosaurs died out, and eventually we began noticing weird old bones and trying to explain them.

People thought that elephant skeletons were actually giants or Cyclopes.

You wouldn't guess that a trunk took up the space in the middle of their skulls, especially if you had never seen anything like an elephant before.

And these skeletons turned up in parts of Europe where it was too cold for an elephant to live.

Griffins were said to have the head of an eagle, the body of a lion, and the tail of a serpent. Sometimes they also had wings.

Protoceratops is about 10 feet long and has a skeleton like this.

The neck frills break very easily.

"Sediment" is basically tiny bits of dirt shifted around by water, wind, ice, and gravity.

As the sediment builds up it protects the remains.

Sedimentary rocks form when layers of sediment build up over time and compress.

Metamorphic rocks form from heat and pressure on other rocks underground.

Igneous rocks form from magma in the Earth's core.

If the buried bone is in a really dry place, like the desert, and no water ever gets to it, it can fossilize unaltered. But this is rare.

MINERAL-RICH WATER

PASSAGE OF TIME

When water reaches the bone, it brings along other minerals, which get sponged up into the bone and harden in a process called permineralization.

The fossil stays hidden until either someone digs down and finds it, or the soil and rock above it erodes away.

In 1800, a lot of fossils were about to find their way to the surface.

In the year 1800...

The Earth is 6,006 years old.

Dinosaurs are known as monsters.

They lived a few thousand years ago.

They disappeared because of Noah's flood.

There are no examples of dinosaurs living at this time.

We are certain about all of this.

HOW DO I GET TO NAME A DINOSAUR?

1. Become a paleontologist,* then discover a new species and write about it.

2. Win a contest! In 2005, the Children's Museum of Indianapolis held a contest to name what became *"Dracorex hogwartsia,"* which means the "Dragon King of Hogwarts."

   *Amateurs can also find and study fossils, but you do have to know all the technical terms for everything and write a scientific paper.

Mary Anning wasn't limited to one spectacular icthyosaur find.

"Lizard fish" kept turning up on the coast of Lyme Regis, along with other creatures.

Two years earlier, Buckland's friend Reverend William Conybeare had found a skull and fin and named it "plesiosaur."

Holy cats! She found it!

Like this one, in December 1823.

Wait! That looks like the Loch Ness monster!

Before then, Nessie was the Greek monster hippocampus...

...which is also a part of your brain.

The first image of Nessie as a plesiosaur is from 1933.

DAILY MAIL
MONSTER SPOTTED

HYPOTHALAMUS

DAILY MAIL
MONSTER SPOTTED
LOCH NESS MONSTER

Anning would find a smaller creature in December 1828, about the size of a raven.

The pterodactyl had first been discovered in Bavaria, in 1784. It wasn't named until 1809 by Georges Cuvier.

I posit that the *Pterodactylus* was not a fish, but *flew!*

It would be the first of its kind found in England.

In 1794, Cuvier was hired as an assistant to the head of comparative anatomy at the Institute of France in Paris.

He soon became one of the most important scientists in Europe.

Cuvier studied every text he could get relating to petrified bones.

"All the facts point towards a world before ours, destroyed by some catastrophe."

Including the legend of Yakwawi, which may be based on mastodon fossils found by Native Americans.

"In Kentucky a battle between Yakwawi and all other animals left the area covered in bones."

People thought no species had ever died out completely.

Even though no one had seen a dodo since 1700.

A frozen mammoth turned up in Siberia soon after Cuvier's paper was published...

...confirming it was no animal that still lived.

Mantell lost out on the discovery of the first dinosaur by one year to William Buckland...

...whose *Megalosaurus* overshadowed the *Iguanodon* in many ways.

Mantell would also find the *Hylaeosaurus*.

Noticing a shared spinal feature on *Iguanodon*, *Megalosaurus*, and *Hylaeosaurus*, a brilliant young anatomist categorized the order "Dinosauria" in 1842.

DEINOS (Greek) adj. terrible, fearfully great, wondrous. [connotes: the unknowable, powerful, awesome.]

SAUROS (Greek) n. a lizard.

Owen

But dinosaurs are *reptiles*— not lizards.

Meh, "Dinoherpeton" sounds weird.

Deino was a Greek monster and one of three sisters, the Graeae. She was related to sea gods, a Cyclops, a dragon with 100 heads, and Medusa.

Her name means "dread."

Reptiles included turtles, snakes, lizards, and crocodiles. They had just been separated from amphibians like frogs and newts.

Ichthyosaurs and plesiosaurs were placed in their own category for marine life.

Pterosaurs were classed in their own order, since no one had figured them out yet.

Pterosauria

Ichthyosauria

Owen wrote a number of insightful papers and established himself as Cuvier's intellectual successor.

HEY!

Then he used his powers to bar other scientists access to research and disparaged their work.

Especially Gideon Mantell.

Mister Buckland, he's completely mischaracterized my *Iguanodon* research! Which I can't even publish, as he controls the Geological Society.

Can it be intentional? How *ungentle-manly!*

It was *indeed ungentlemanly!* Buckland himself was guilty of failing to credit Mary Anning in his papers, as were all his contemporaries who used her finds in their work.

I am most ill used by these men of science, Miss Pliney.

But Owen would undo himself when he won the Royal Medal of the Royal Society for research on a type of extinct squid that had been presented at the Geological Society four years before by someone else.

I call it Belemnites owenni!

Owen began to lose face for his plagiarism, but continued to be a butthead.

Well, really, that's not right! There's no animal alive that makes its stomach work against gravity!

What a gross misuse of energy!

IGUANODON

When Mantell died, Owen published an obituary of Mantell dismissing all his scientific contributions, but praising his own work.

His venemous hatred for Mantell and inflated ego began to ostracize Owen from his peers.

WHAM

Owen was ousted from his positions in the Geological and Royal Societies, the leading scientific organizations of the day.

But in the regular world, Owen was still thought of as a great scientist.

Her Majesty Queen Victoria and Prince Albert.

In his later years, Owen would work to make the British Museum accessible to the working man, which is perhaps his best scientific legacy.

Although these representations would be out of fashion in a few decades, the original statues can still be seen in Sydenham Park, London.

In the year 1854...

The Earth is 400,000 years old.

Dinosaurs are known as extinct reptiles.

They lived hundreds of thousands of years ago.

They disappeared for unknown reasons.

There are no examples of dinosaurs living today.

We are certain about all of this.

HOW DO DINOSAURS GET NAMED?

They're often named with a descriptive phrase in Greek or Latin, though lately Chinese and Mongolian descriptions have been used as well.

Mirischia means "wonderful pelvis," because of its asymmetric hips.

Yinlong means "Hidden Dragon," and refers to the movie *Crouching Tiger, Hidden Dragon*, which was filmed near where the fossils were discovered.

Sometimes it's for the place where it was discovered.

Nqwebasaurus was found in the Nqweba region of South Africa.

Fukuiraptor is the "thief of the Fukui province" of Japan.

Muttaburrasaurus is from Australia.

Gojirasaurus was named after Godzilla, using the original Japanese pronunciation.

Sometimes they just get a weird name, like *Irritator*, whose specimen was a skull with plaster added to it, which annoyed the scientists who studied it.

Charles Darwin published *The Origin of the Species* in 1859 to acclaim and controversy. It proposed the theory of evolution.

Species diverge over the generations as offspring living in different habitats inherit different beneficial traits from earlier generations.

How far out was this idea?

Darwin

Mainly Seed Eating

Mainly Insect Eating

Cactus Seeds and Parts

Ancestral Ground Finch

Buds and Fruits

Adaptive Radiation In Galápagos Finches

48

The jealousy between Cope and Marsh made them rush to make discoveries before each other, and led to some mistakes.

Their biggest: *Brontosaurus*, the most famous dinosaur that never existed.*

In Loving Memory

What's up, guys?

This is so awkward. You tell him.

Brontosaurus was a mash-up of two different Sauropod species.

I'm not gonna tell him. You tell him.

Marsh's crew found a mostly complete apatosaur skeleton, minus the skull.

So Marsh put a *Camarasaurus* skull from three miles away on top.

*OR SO WE THOUGHT. See pg 112

53

Ornithiscians include these types:

Ceratopsians (with frills)

Hadrosaurs (or duck-billed dinosaurs)

Ankylosaurs and Stegosaurs (the armored dinosaurs)

Pachycephalosaurs (head butters)

Sauriscians include:

Sauropods

Theropods

Dinosaurs were also divided based on their diets—whether they ate meat or plants.

The plant eaters, or herbivores, tend to have a more beak-shaped jaw to pull leaves off of branches or plants out of the ground.

Their teeth are flat on the end to grind plants.

The meat eaters, or carnivores, need their jaws to slice through animal skin and muscle to pull it off of bones.

They have teeth that are more knife-shaped, sometimes with serrated edges like a steak knife.

Herbivores mostly ate leaves, ferns, and matter from coniferous trees in the Triassic and Jurassic periods. Flowering and fruiting plants (which include every vegetable) did not appear until about 140 million years ago.

Some herbivorous species have been found with gastroliths near their abdomen— small rocks that helped grind up the plants inside the dinosaurs' stomachs.

Today we're familiar with this digestion technique in birds.

GRIND GRIND GRIND GRIND GRIND GRIND

Ostriches are attracted to shiny pebbles and stones for this purpose, and have been known to swallow people's jewelry and watches!

Darwin's friend Thomas Huxley viewed *Archaeopteryx* as an evolutionary link between dinosaurs and birds.

Owen naturally disagreed. He'd classed it as a bird and never admitted to making mistakes.

Huxley visited America and met with Marsh in 1877. Marsh was working on a book about "Odontornithes"— birds with teeth!

Besides having similar skeletons, the internal bone structure also looked like a bird's.

They both had pneumatic bone that could fill with air.

Except for *Archaeopteryx*, most people considered dinosaurs to be cold-blooded reptiles.

Not me! I've always thought they were warm-blooded!

Except for Richard Owen.

Baron Franz Nopcsa of Transylvania agreed a generation later. He saw many anatomical similarities in the skeletons of theropods and birds.

Nopcsa

He began studying bones his sister found on their family estate in what is now Romania.

He served as a spy for Austria-Hungary during World War I.

Nopcsa also studied the Albanian people.

In 1919, he became the first person to hijack a plane.

After the war, he proposed he be made king of Albania.

Auction the queenship to an American millionaire's daughter. I'll marry her and the money will fund our glorious country.

Nopsca was the first paleobiologist. He tried to reconstruct the ecology of the area to figure out how dinos had lived.

Nopcsa noticed his local dinosaurs were smaller than similar types in other locations.

He determined that the Haţeg area had been an island millions of years before, and the limited space kept down the size they could grow to.

DINO ISLAND

This became known as the "island rule," or the theory of insular dwarfism. Smaller habitat = smaller animals.

USTRIAN EMPIRE

But Transylvania was surrounded by land.

POLAND

MOLDAVIA

TRANSYLVANIA

OTTOMAN EMPIRE

BLACK SEA

WALLACHIA

Wegener published his book on "*Kontinentalverschiebung,*" or continental drift, in 1915.

He thought there had been a primal "Urkontinent" where most of the land was joined in one mass.

Eurasia

Panthalassa Ocean

North America

Paleo-Tethys Ocean

South America

Africa

India

Antarctica

Australia

Wegener wasn't sure how it worked, just that it happened. But he didn't have a geologic background.

He's a weatherman. *A weather-man!!* Don't let him tell us our science!

For the continents to move that far, the Earth had to be pretty old.

The oldest estimates came from physicist Lord Kelvin at somewhere between 24 - 400 million years, and we didn't really know enough about the Earth to calculate its age.

In the year 1920...

The Earth is as much as 400 million years old.

Dinosaurs are known as extinct reptiles.

They lived 3 million years ago.

They disappeared because they lost the survival of the fittest.

There are no examples of dinosaurs living today.

We are certain about all this.

The first woman to write a scientific paper about a dinosaur discovery was Professor Mignon Talbot of Mount Holyoke College.

Talbot

In 1911, she discovered a nearly complete *Podokesaurus holyokensis*, missing only the head.

But ten years later, the only specimen burned down in a fire at the museum. Fortunately a cast survives in Yale's Peabody Museum in New Haven.

In the early 1920s, the American Museum of Natural History in New York began a series of explorations into the Gobi Desert in Mongolia.

Mongolia is geographically unique, sandwiched between China and Russia, two countries that were full of turmoil and political upheaval in the early part of the 20th century.

During World War I, Roy Chapman Andrews spied on these countries for the US, under the guise of collecting animal specimens for the Museum of Natural History.

Don't mind me. I'm definitely just here to shoot your wildlife!

Say, where have you boys been lately? Seen anything neat?

After the war, Andrews convinced the museum (and a number of millionaire backers from New York) to let him lead a team of cars and camels into the Gobi to explore the desert's geology and ecology.

Simply anyone who's *anyone* is backing Andrews. He's such a dapper fellow!

All right, Andrews, I'm game for a grand.

Thank you! Please make out the check to the natural history museum!

In the Gobi, Andrews found the first dinosaur eggs.

The crew found a lot of ceratopsian skeletons around the site, and when they found a skeleton among the eggs...

They named it oviraptor— egg thief.

The expedition also discovered the *Velociraptor!*

The museum made about 5 trips to the Gobi during 1923-30, but encountered increasing problems. Political unrest from revolutions happening in each country also complicated the trips.

We need to avoid the soldiers if we want to keep our supplies.

Mongolia was taken over by Russia, and an expedition there became far too bureaucratic and expensive for the museum to finance.

WE WANT WORK NOW!

UNEMPLOYED WILL TAKE ANY JOB

WILL TAKE ANY JOB

WANTED ANY JOB 2 YEARS 16 YEAR

WANTED JOB CLEAN

GIVE MY DAD A JOB

The Great Depression and then World War II turned a lot of focus onto physics and nuclear research.

This rocky portion of history prevented much paleontology and geology from being done.

But some geology was squeezed in, thanks to Princeton mineralogist Harry Hess, who left the fathometer on his submarine running day and night through out the war.

Yes, sir!

Keep up the good work, Hess, the Nazis could be on us at any moment!

He found that the Atlantic was full of canyons and valleys, which meant that it was (geologically speaking) very young.

An ancient floor that was static would have filled up with silt and mud at the bottom and been smooth instead of craggy.

After the war and throughout the '50s, oceanographers explored the Atlantic more and discovered a rift in the middle.

They dated rocks from different points and found that the farther from the rift you got, the older the rocks got.

So smooth!

I'm stayin' put right here, dagnabbit!

TO THE RIFT

Toward the rift, they got younger, which meant the rift was spreading the seafloor apart.

74

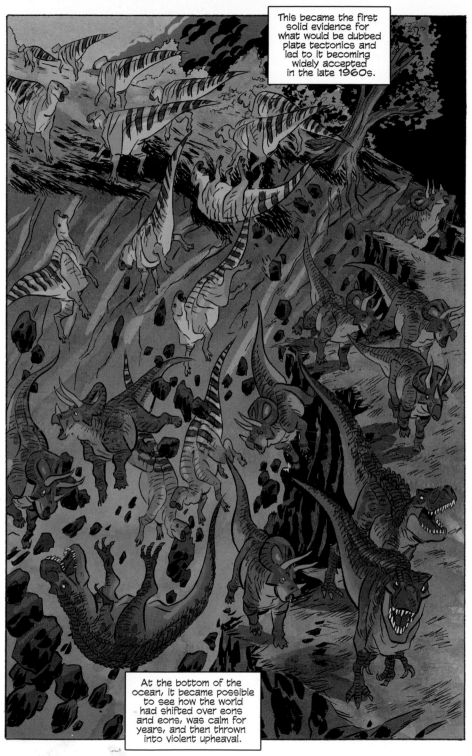

This became the first solid evidence for what would be dubbed plate tectonics and led to it becoming widely accepted in the late 1960s.

At the bottom of the ocean, it became possible to see how the world had shifted over eons and eons, was calm for years, and then thrown into violent upheaval.

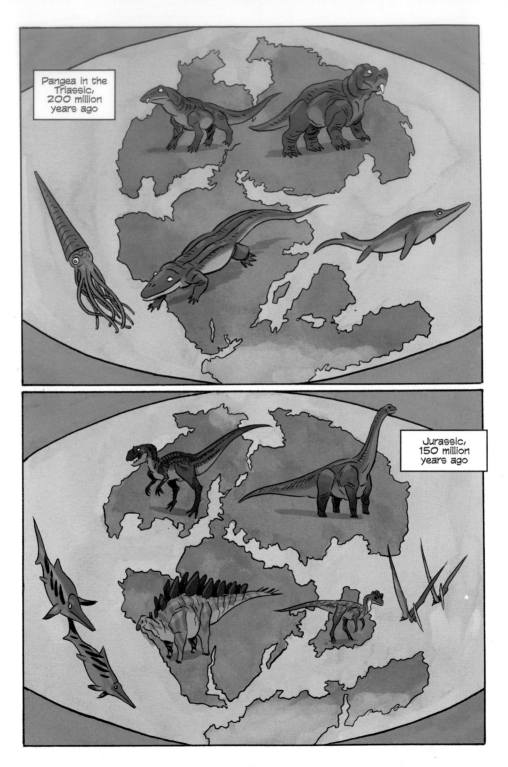

Pangea in the Triassic, 200 million years ago

Jurassic, 150 million years ago

Cretaceous, 70 million years ago

Modern-Day Earth

For 40 years, few dinosaur discoveries had been made in the West, but lots of work had been happening in Asia. The USSR, which now included Mongolia, sent teams back into the Gobi, and in 1971, a Polish/Mongolian expedition found the skeleton of a *Velociraptor* and *Protoceratops* locked in combat.

These two may have been fighting when a sandstorm buried them alive.

Or the *Velociraptor* might have been scavenging the remains.

But fighting dinosaurs were about to become a hot topic.

Because it takes a lot of energy to fight.

And high-energy activity points to endothermy, an ability to create your own heat internally, instead of relying on external heat.

Ectotherms, or cold-blooded animals, rely on warm temperatures to produce enough heat for a lot of activity. They tend to live in more tropical climates. If most of your activity is eating leaves, then you don't necessarily need as much speed.

It's getting so hot out here, I'm gonna put my sail up!

'Cause that's how we cool down.

Plus if you're a multistory-tall sauropod, you don't worry much about hiding, running away, or anything that's smaller than you.

Discoveries like *Deinonychus* in 1964 inspired some new thoughts on the internal processes of dinosaurs.

And some movie villains.

Clever girl.

Jack Horner put more dents in the cold-blooded theory with his *Maiasaura* nest studies in Montana in the '70s.

He had stumbled into a roadside rock shop housed in a former church run by Marion Brandvold, an amateur fossil hunter.

ROCK SHOP

She'd found the first baby dinosaur nests in North America in the land near her home, which she regularly explored with her family.

The bones they found were too large to have recently hatched from the eggs in the nest: about 16 inches long, ranging to almost 5 feet long.

They grew that big over the course of a year, which is a good indicator of a high metabolism and endothermy.

Their size, worn teeth, and the bones of fully grown maiasaurs nearby indicated that the babies were being fed by their parents.

Their eyes and nostrils were also larger compared to adults, (scientifically referred to as "cuteness"), which happens in animals raised by their parents, making their babies look more helpless.

We started to find more nests, like titanosaurs', who, for obvious reasons, did *not* sit on their eggs.

They let heat released from decaying plants keep their eggs warm.

In 1993, new Mongolian nest finds were uncovered, this time with fossilized embryos that let us look inside the egg.

The eggs that were supposed to be *Protoceratops* actually belonged to the egg thief, *Oviraptor!*

The dinosaur that we thought had been trying to snack on eggs was really incubating them.

FOOOSH

A nest was found where an *Oviraptor* had spread its wings over the eggs, protecting them until it died.

We assumed that because dinosaurs were reptilian, they left their eggs behind like reptiles.

WE'RE FREE!

But we kept uncovering more and more similarities with birds.

They had similar bones. And feet.

They lay eggs in nests, and used gastroliths in their stomach to help break up food.

And it was really easy to see a link between a small theropod like *Velociraptor* and a crane or ostrich.

And there were birds like the extinct moa that were huge—12 feet high!

And cassowaries, who live in Austrailia, are big, have a fierce claw on their middle toe, and have been known to injure and kill people.

But in meteorites, it's much more common.

They eventually found the site of the impact in Chicxulub, Mexico, buried under hundreds of feet of soil.

The object that hit Earth was bigger than one of Mars's moons, Deimos.

Deimos, incidentally, also means "dread" in Greek, and with his twin, Phobos, he would follow their father, the god Ares, into battle.

The blast was about three times as powerful as an atomic bomb.

Anything near it would have been killed instantly.

For the next four months, the air had so much soot in it, no sun could reach through.

Plants died out, and food was scarce for everyone.

We now think the impact came at a particularly bad time for dinos. Sea levels had fallen, and the ecology of the surrounding areas was devastated.

And intense volcanic activity in India didn't help.

It's possible that if it had happened at a more peaceful time in their history, some dinosaur species would have survived the impact.

Utahraptor

Deinonychus

Velociraptor

Scientists began to wonder if this meant *all* dinosaurs had been feathered...

Aw, I used to look so tough!

PUNK ROCK FOR LIFE!!!

YEAH!

You're still totally fierce.

KRRK

...or just those few that had been found with feathers.

It's hard to tell because skin and soft tissue rarely are preserved for us to find.

It seemed like we had narrowed it down to theropods.

HA HA HA HA HA HA HA HA HA HA HA

AW, THAT'S *STILL* ME!

Then we found a feathered *Kulindadromeus* in Siberia, which is ornithischian and not saurischian like theropods.

If both branches had feathers (or some earlier form of them), then feathers evolved with an earlier common ancestor.

92

In the year 2000...

The Earth is 4.5 billion years old.

Dinosaurs are known as extinct reptilian ancestors of birds.

They lived 250 to 65 million years ago.

They disappeared because an asteroid impact devastated their ecology.

There are descendants of dinosaurs living today.

We are pretty sure about all of this.

HOW BIG WERE DINOSAURS AND THEIR RELATIVES?

Quetzalcoatlus had a wingspan of 45 feet, the largest creature to ever fly. Its wingspan was as long as a semitrailer.

Argentinosaurus was 120 feet long and almost 100 tons, the weight of 12 elephants.

Sauroposeidon was the tallest, 56 feet high, 3 times the height of a giraffe!

Spinosaurus was the biggest carnivore, almost 60 feet long— as long as a bowling alley lane.

Shantungosaurus is the biggest ornithischian, 50 feet long and up to 50 tons!

Epidexipteryx was the smallest adult, 10 inches long and 1/3 of a pound—about the weight of a hockey puck.

In every country with
rock old enough,
they turn up, including
islands like Madagascar,
Japan, and New Zealand.

Cryolophosaurus was a therapod found in Antarctica that may have had night vision for hunting during the long Antarctic nights.

Deinocheirus had arms that were over 8 feet long and was thought to be omnivorous.

Oryctodromeus was a burrowing dinosaur, a behavior we only discovered a decade ago.

Some species, like *Psittacosaurus*, may have had older offspring guard nests while parents searched for food, a behavior that's seen today in certain species of birds, like crows.

Mamenchisaurus and *Supersaurus* were sauropods whose necks made up half their body size and were over one hundred feet long.

Spinosaurs were massive, maybe the biggest carnivorous dinosaur, and hunted in water and on land.

Computers have made it easier to analyze data and visualize bodies. We began to compare dinosaur tracks with dinosaur feet and leg fossils, and can figure out how fast they moved.

We can also use computer models to figure out how hard a tail could smack another dinosaur in the face.

Back off, *creep!*

We examined the airflow inside skulls like *Stegoceras's* and figured out how strong their smell receptors were.

Take a bath, *bro!*

KRAK

THUD

Some of our experiments with computer modeling do look pretty silly.

We put fake butts on chickens to simulate how theropods walked with a bigger tail.

104

We're unsure how many different kinds of dinosaurs there are. Scientists have named 1,300 species in 300 genera right now, but that number might only be as low as 800. Revisions are being made constantly.

Not every dinosaur died when it was a full-grown adult. Some were babies, some were teenagers, and some got to be pretty old. And they looked very different at each of these ages.

Triceratops Juvenile

Baby *Triceratops*

Triceratops Adult

Baby

Juvenile

Adult

We can determine a dinosaur's age when it died by looking at its bone density under a microscope. Young bone is spongy; older bone is dense.

Based on studies from Dr. Anusuya Chinsamy-Turan.

We can also determine how fast the bone grew from the structures left behind, and that not all dinosaurs grew at the same rate. Some, like *Triceratops*, grew over their entire lives.

There may have been skeletal differences in each gender's appearance that we haven't figured out yet.

And some fossils have been found that weren't complete skeletons. Sometimes a femur or some teeth is all that remains, and we might never find another example of it existing.

And sometimes we lose fossils and can't compare new finds to old ones. There are some missing Cope and Marsh fossils we'll *never* see.

Argentinosaurus

Gorgosaurus

—NOTES—

p. 34   Plesiosaurs are no longer part of Ichthyosauria.

p. 51   The validity of *Agathaumas* as a genus is debated.

p. 51   *Edaphosaurus* lived in the late Carboniferous to early Permian periods (around 300 to 275 million years ago), 25 million years prior to the Mesozoic era, when dinosaurs lived. It predates dinosaurs, and it's an earlier ancestor to both dinosaurs and mammals.

p. 59   The original name for this specimen was *Archaeopteryx siemensii,* but it is commonly referred to as "the Berlin Specimen." As *A. siemensii* is the first name in the record, *A. owenni* is invalid.

p. 60   The Odontornithes book would later be called a waste of taxpayer money in Congress and used to oust Marsh from the US Geological Survey. It was a huge scandal.

p. 65   This explanation is slightly simplified; one isotope of uranium decays to another isotope at a steady rate, and the ratio between them is what's actually measured.

p. 70   Roy Chapman Andrews's spying mostly involved reporting on the political climate of the countries he visited back to the United States. He was more of a field reporter than a James Bond type, but Andrews is part of the inspiration for Indiana Jones. He wrote several books about his adventures and discoveries, and was the subject of comics in the 1950s as well.

—GLOSSARY—

Avian dinosaur
    birds, after discovering they are descended from dinosaurs

Carnivore
    Animal that eats meat

Cololite
    Fecal matter inside the intestines/body that has been fossilized

Coprolite
    Fecal matter that has been excreted and has been fossilized

Ectotherm
    Animals that absorb heat from their environment, also referred to as cold-blooded

Endotherm
    Animals that create their own internal heat, also referred to as warm-blooded

Fossil
    A previously living thing that has been preserved in sediment and turned into rock over a very long time, or an impression left in rock by something once alive

Herbivore
    Animal that eats plants

Non-avian dinosaur
any species of *Dinosauria* except for the clade of Aves; every dinosaur that isn't a bird

Omnivore
Animal that eats both plants and meat

Paleontology
The study of fossilized animals and plants

Permineralization
The process through which living tissue becomes a fossil, involving the absorption and hardening of minerals

Petrification
The process through which organic matter becomes hard like stone

Sediment
Very tiny pieces of dirt and rocks

Strata
Layers of sediment that can be told apart by changes in color and texture due to variations in their components over thousands of years

PERMIAN

JURASSIC

CRETACEOUS

TRIASSIC

C E N O Z O I C	HOLOCENE	10,000 YEARS
	PLEISTOCENE	1.8
	PLIOCENE	5.3
	MIOCENE	23
	OLIGOCENE	33.9
	EOCENE	55.8
	PALEOCENE	65.5
M E S O Z O I C	CRETACEOUS	145.5
	JURASSIC	199.6
	TRIASSIC	252.5
P A L E O Z O I C	PERMIAN	299
	PENNSYLVANIAN	318
	MISSISSIPPIAN	359.2
	DEVONIAN	416
	SILURIAN	443
	ORDOVICIAN	488.3
	CAMBRIAN	542

Millions of years

—FURTHER READING—

Ottaviani, Jim, and Big Time Attic. *Bone Sharps, Cowboys, and Thunder Lizards*. Ann Arbor, MI: General Tektronics Labs, 2005.

Lambert, David. *Eyewitness Books: Dinosaur*. New York: DK Publishing, 2010.

Benton, Professor Mike. *The Kingfisher Dinosaur Encyclopedia*. New York: Macmillan, 2010.

Holtz, Dr. Thomas R., Jr., and Luis V. Rey. *Dinosaurs*. New York: Random House Children's Books, 2007.